Child Alters

Shirley J. Davis

Contents

Introduction..6

What Is Dissociative Identity Disorder 7

Dissociative Identity Disorder in the DSM 5............11

An Explanation of the Diagnostic Criteria of
Dissociative Identity Disorder 13

Where Does the Term Dissociative Identity Disorder
come from? 23

Leaving Self-Hatred Behind...................................28

Self-Love 35

Methods to Cultivate Self-Love.................................37

Child Alters: A Blast from the Past.........................40

Trauma-Time 41

The Concept of the Inner Child 46

The Benefits of Knowing Your Inner Child 49

Recognizing Your Wounded Inner Child 52

The Wounds of Neglect Experienced by Inner
Children 56

What are Child Alters? 60

Trauma Time..63

ANPs and EPs..67

How Do Child Alters Form?.......................................71

Healing Child Alters 74

Inner Child Work..75

Beginning the Healing Journey: Understanding Psychological Trauma.................................80

Brain Changes Brought on by Psychological Trauma
....83

Working with Child Alters 91

Re-parenting Oneself..96

Forms of Reparenting 102

Learning to Love Child Alters 107

Beginning an Inner Dialogue with Alters 108

Enjoy Your Inner Children....................................114

References...115

Lists of Links to Helpful Websites..........................118

Introduction

The subject of child alters has been one that has consistently popped up in my emails from readers of my blog, www.learnaboutdidcom.

Because of this interest, I wrote a book to outline what I know from experience and online research about child alters, what they are, how to treat them, and how to deal with them when they become unruly.

Although I am not a licensed mental health professional, I believe those living with the diagnosis of dissociative identity disorder will gain much insight into their inner children.

This insight will aid in healing because readers will no longer feel afraid or jealous of these little parts of themselves.

Good luck on your healing journey.

Shirley J. Davis

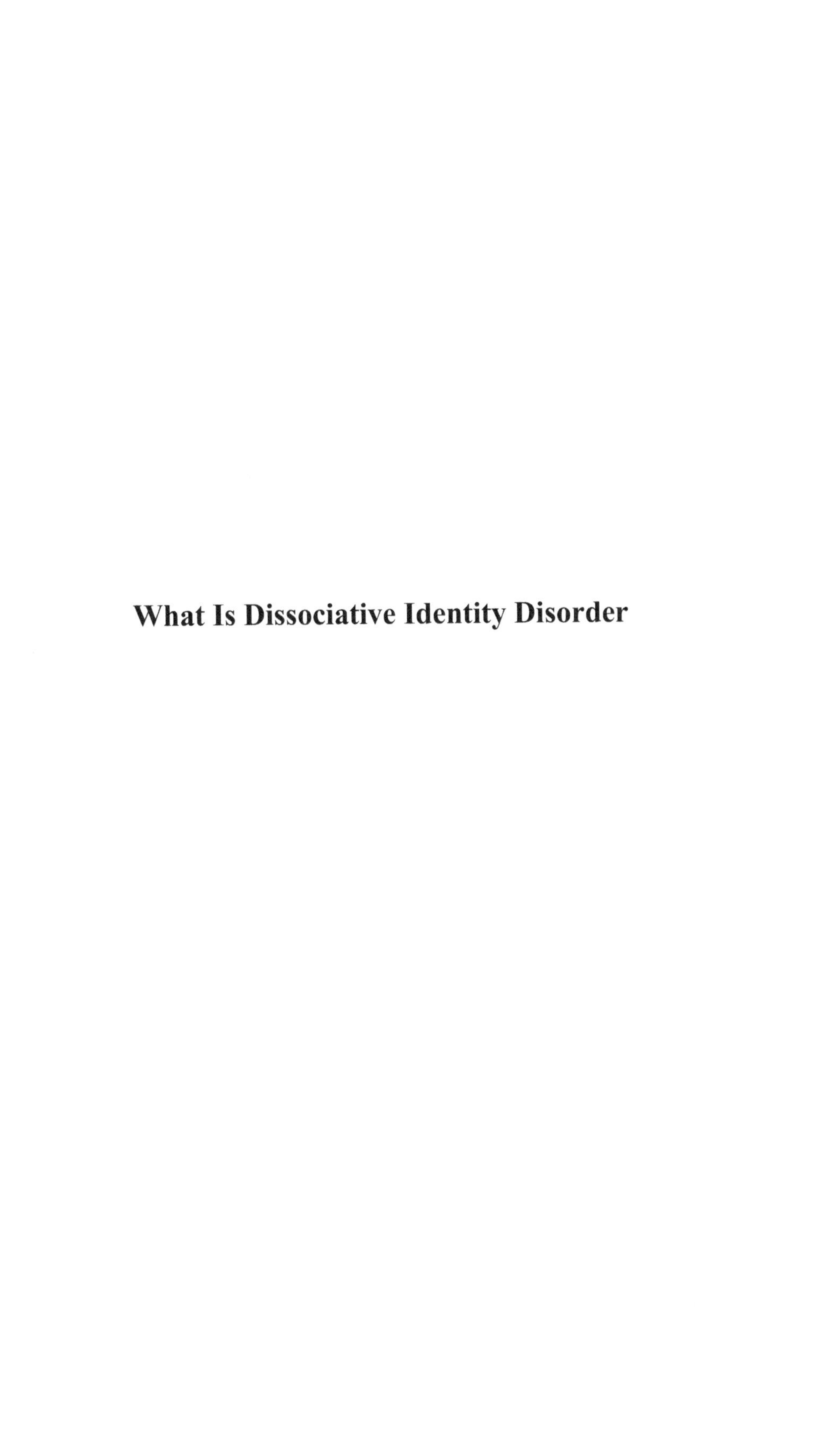

What Is Dissociative Identity Disorder

No book about child alters would be complete without first discussing what dissociative identity disorder (DID) is and how it is treated.

Dissociative identity disorder is a developmental condition that is characterized by alternating multiple identity states. These states, also known as parts, alters, and inner people, can temporarily take over the body of the multiple (person who has DID) and wreak havoc on their life.

It is estimated that 1 in every 1000 people living in the United States has DID but the condition could be wider spread than that as misdiagnosis is normal. In fact, it takes someone who has dissociative identity disorder 11 years or more to receive the correct diagnosis and treatment.

Dissociative identity disorder has for far too long been treated like a nonsense diagnosis. However, it is a recognized diagnostic condition in the Diagnostic and Statistical Manual of Mental Disorders, 5th Edition: DSM-5, the bible of the psychiatric world.

The controversy over the diagnosis seems to arise because some clinicians do not want to recognize that one person could endure so much trauma and still be sane and alive.

However, people have endured the trauma that survivors with DID have for as long as humanity has been on the planet and cases of people struggling with multiple states of consciousness are reported and documented as far back as the 1815.

Dissociative identity disorder forms in very young children whose brains have not fully formed and whose personality is still pliable as the result of severe and repeated trauma.

These traumatic events may encompass many kinds of abuse, including:

- Sexual abuse
- Physical abuse
- Emotional abuse
- Narcissistic abuse
- Child neglect
- Abandonment of a child

These traumatic events cause cortisol levels to rise in abused and neglected children to ready them for the fight/flight/freeze/fawn response. However, these cortisol levels never are allowed to return to baseline because of the unpredictable behaviors of the child's abusers. These higher than average cortisol levels interfere with the child's ability to meet developmental milestones.

One of these vital developmental milestones is that of coalescing into one coherent and whole personality. More on this later.

Dissociative Identity Disorder in the DSM 5

There have been many iterations of the Diagnostic Manual of Mental Disorders, published by the American Psychiatric Association, but it wasn't until the DSM-4 that we find DID listed with its own criteria, making it separate from other dissociative disorders.

There are five criteria for diagnosing dissociative identity disorder, including:

A. Disruption of identity characterized by two or more distinct personality states, which may be described in some cultures as an experience of possession. The disruption of marked discontinuity in the sense of self and sense of agency, accompanied by related alterations in effect, behavior, consciousness, memory, perception, cognition, and/or sensory-motor functioning. These signs and symptoms may be observed by others or reported by the individual.

B. Recurrent gaps in the recall of everyday events, important personal information, and/or traumatic events that are inconsistent with ordinary forgetting.

C. The symptoms cause clinically significant distress or impairment in social, occupational, or other key areas of functioning.

D. The disturbance is not a normal part of a broadly accepted cultural or religious practice. Note: In children, the symptoms are not better explained by imaginary playmates or other fantasy play.

E. The symptoms are not because of the physiological effects of a substance (e.g., blackouts or chaotic behavior during alcohol intoxication) or another medical condition (e.g., complex partial seizures).

Because of the DSM 5, dissociative identity disorder is a recognized mental health condition and can now be treated without a clinician feeling they are going against the grain.

However, there are some mental health professionals who still will not recognize the diagnosis even though it is a valid diagnosis.

An Explanation of the Diagnostic Criteria of Dissociative Identity Disorder

Criteria A: Distinct Personality States.

Criteria A: A person diagnosed with Dissociative Identity Disorder has "distinct personality states."

Criteria A is describing the phenomenon of the presence of alternate ego states often called simply alters or parts. Alters may consist of fully developed parts and fragments of parts. They may be children and adults of all ages, sexes, sexual orientations, and have different tastes in many things.

Except for a few people, alters do not readily show themselves to strangers or even to their therapists. Trust must be engendered before any of a system will be overt or "out" and be recognizable as not the person normally in control of the body.

Thankfully, a change placed in the DSM-5 makes it easier to diagnose DID without the clinician having to directly observe a switch between alters.

Instead, DID can be confidently diagnosed with self-reports of the presence and effects of alternate ego states, or of another person's description of seeing a switch between alters.

Two clusters of symptoms show alters if they are not observed.

These are described in the DSM-5's extended description of Dissociative Identity Disorder: Sudden alterations or discontinuities in the sense of self and sense of agency (Criteria A), and recurrent dissociative amnesias (Criteria B).

Sense of Self

The term "sense of self" is used in the DSM's Dissociative Identity Disorder Criterion A, and describes distinct personality states, better known as alter personalities. A discontinuity in a person's sense of self can drastically affect any part of the person's functioning.

There are many differences felt among the varying alter ego states.

Attitudes, outlooks, and personal preferences like preferred foods or clothes may change and can be radically different. This is especially true because many of the alters are of different ages and sexes. These alter ego states are often not aware of each other's existence or are aware of only a few others. For them, the body is theirs and no one else.

Sense of Agency

Alters can also strongly influence the behavior of the waking self, even when not triggered. Their emotions and thoughts are constantly intruding into the consciousness of the waking self, presenting as voices or even images in the mirror.

When that alter is no longer active, everything changes back until the next time the same alter is triggered. At first, the waking self may feel disoriented to time and place and experience confusion. After gaining their bearings, the person may find they are wearing or have in their closet clothes they would not normally buy or wear.

They may find their credit or debit card has been used, but they do not know by whom. The person may feel like they do not have control of their lives, feelings, thoughts, or feelings. Often, it is this symptom that drives these people to therapy because they believe they are going insane.

Switching

Switching from one alter state to another can happen unexpectedly and with or with no one else noticing. Only in DID can a person switch so drastically from one alter ego state to another, where the alter takes over their bodies.

Outside of treatment, many people experience switching but do not know it is abnormal to do so. They assume that since they have been experiencing lost time and not remembering things they have said and done, it is something everyone does. It is their baseline, their normal.

It is a great surprise to find out that what they have been experiencing is considered abnormal.

The waking self may report to their doctor or therapist feelings of watching themselves from the outside or above while "someone else" controls their body. They will hear themselves saying things that are abnormal for them to say and have not the ability to stop it. This is depersonalization taken to the extreme.

Some who live with dissociative identity disorder might think they have been possessed because of experiencing their body and will be "kidnapped" from them. A person with dissociative identity disorder may experience themselves as feeling they are growing taller, shorter, younger, older, or any range of demographic changes.

Recurrent Amnesia: Criterion B

People who live with DID may or not remember the actions of their alters. It is possible for a person to be knowledgeable of their actions while in a dissociated state. Total amnesia for the things done while dissociated is more the norm, however. This discontinuity of behavior and lack of knowing what happened leads friends, relatives, and acquaintances baffled, and when they tell the person of their behaviors and actions, they claim not to know what the reporters are talking about.

Although they are speaking the truth, they can be incorrectly believed to be lying. There are several ways this amnesia can present.

Gaps in memory of personal life events

The person may know that someone has died, but they have no memory of the event, or the subsequent visitation, burial, or funeral.

This can mean the amnesiac has lost four to six days of life to a traumatic event. There is at least one case, and there is probably more of a woman waking up married. This sounds like a joke from a B movie, but it is not funny to the woman or her new husband.

Gaps of memory of other life events that are meaningful can be lost to amnesia as well, including their childhoods, adolescence, or the birth of their children.

Amnesia for events does not need to be only attached to traumatic events, as lapses in dependable memory of what happened during the day today or remembering how to do well-known skills such as driving or reading can inexplicably disappear.

The above symptom applies to the entire person. For example, they may have a child alter who does not know how to drive, or a teen alter who does not understand that a debit card is not bottomless.

Dissociative Fugues

This means a person in an altered state, will travel to another place, are common experiences of people living with dissociative identity disorder. They will 'come to' and find themselves in places they do not remember going to, such as a restaurant, on a date with a stranger, or even in another state.

Sometimes, because these fugue states can last for days or even months, people experiencing a fugue state are reported missing by their families.

If all the gaps in memory for the past or present do not occur, but all the other criteria are met, then the person can be sometimes diagnosed with a sister disorder to DID, Other Dissociative Identity Disorder Presentation.

Clinically Significant Distress or Impairment: Criteria C

The entire criteria of C include:
The symptoms cause clinically significant distress or impairment in social, occupational, or other key areas of functioning.

What the term "that excludes normal reactions to psychosocial stress" means it that the person is having severe problems in their lives with the social, work, and in other ways without the average day-to-day stressors all people face.

As one can imagine, it is exceedingly difficult to manage life, not knowing from day to day who you will become and what you will do. The chaos, as described in a later chapter, is an experience almost too hard to describe.

Money comes up missing, bills do not get paid, and unexplained absenteeism from work all makes life unbearable.

Criteria D: The Disturbance is not a part of a normal cultural or religious practice

Criteria D includes trances, or other religious practices, such as speaking in tongues, which are part of some religious practices. It also includes the fantasies of children, such as imaginary friends or fantasy play.

.

Criteria E: Symptoms are not because of substance abuse or other medical condition

There are symptoms of substance abuse, such as alcohol or psychogenic drugs, that are not a symptom of DID. However, many people who live with DID do have co-occurring and ongoing problems with the abuse of substances, and this can make it difficult to recognize and treat their disorder. There are a few medical conditions that are seen that can be misunderstood and lead to a false diagnosis. Those include complex and partial seizures.

Complex seizures can last up to two minutes and include, among other things, becoming unaware of one's surroundings and wandering behavior.

Partial Seizures can cause the person to suddenly look blank, also commonly observed with DID (American Psychiatric Association, 2013).

Where Does the Term Dissociative Identity Disorder come from?

Dissociative identity disorder was once known as multiple personality disorder. However, as research has continued into the diagnosis, it was realized that the term multiple personality disorder did not fit.

No one has more than one personality. In DID, a person has one personality that did not come together as one in early childhood, a milestone that occurs between the ages of 5 and 7 years.

In 1990, the psychiatric establishment finally realized that multiple personality disorder was an unrealistic diagnosis and renamed it dissociative identity disorder.

DID is a trauma-driven diagnosis having deep roots in traumatic (abusive) events in childhood. Trauma is the endgame of extraordinarily stressful events that breaks a person's sense of being secure. Distress makes you feel helpless and like you are living in a world that is far too dangerous.

Trauma may leave its victims struggling with negative and upsetting emotions, memories, and sometimes crushing anxiety, leaving people feeling numb and disconnected.

Traumatic events often involve some type of threat to life and/or safety, leaving one feeling overwhelmed and isolated. It is not the circumstances that determine whether an event is traumatic, but a person's emotional experience of that event that makes it traumatic. Thus, an event can be traumatic with or without physical harm.

The more frightened one feels during the traumatic event, the more helpless the victim feels.

Everyone behaves differently when confronted with traumatic events. Because we are so different from one another, we shouldn't judge our reactions concerning how others react.

There are two types of symptoms for trauma, emotional and physical, and both types are often experienced by those living with dissociative identity disorder.

Emotional Symptoms:

- Shock, denial, or disbelief
- Anger, irritability,
- Confusion, difficulty concentrating
- Anxiety and fear
- Withdrawing from others
- Guilt, shame, and self-blame
- Feeling disconnected or numb
- A sense that you do not belong in the world

Physical Symptoms:

- Fatigue
- Insomnia
- Nightmares
- Easily startled,
- Racing heartbeat
- Edginess and agitation
- Unexplained pain
- Muscle tension

People who have DID also live with complex post-traumatic stress disorder and face a long uphill climb to health.

No matter the symptoms or reactions to traumatic events, people living with DID are totally normal for where they have been and what they have endured.

The consensus is that dissociative identity disorder is caused by repeated and highly traumatic events, such as childhood sexual abuse, childhood physical abuse, severe neglect, and mental abuse, including narcissistic abuse.

Ask anyone who has DID, and they will confirm that they are experiencing the emergence of horrific memories of events from their past. These traumatic events change their life paths, leading to losses too many to recount here.

All children are dissociated and do not have a firm personality during the first five to seven years of life. Dissociative identity disorder forms when a child's psychological development is disrupted by early, repetitive trauma. The child's normal process of consolidating a core sense of self-identity is disrupted, leaving the child dissociated.

Because of overwhelming trauma, children develop multiple and conflicting self-states or identities, mirroring the radical contradictions in their early social and family environments.

Often, among the self-states that a multiple encounters on their healing journey, many are children.

Leaving Self-Hatred Behind

One of the long-lasting complications of living through abuse and neglect in children is that survivors grow into adults who strongly dislike themselves. This self-hate is filled with feelings of guilt, inadequacy, and low self-esteem, with survivors continually comparing themselves to others.

These folks also will ignore the positives about themselves and instead pay close attention to any perceived flaws. This self-loathing is misplaced as survivors are not responsible for what happened to them and have absolutely no control over the events that took place.

Self-loathing can inhibit working with child alters.

People who don't love themselves feel they can never be *good enough* and are worthless to themselves, their families, and society. But why? Why do survivors struggle with self-loathing? The pain of self-hatred can be because of many reasons, including childhood trauma, which can prevent the development of the self and self-esteem, perfectionism in the home, which leads children to believe they will never be good enough. Sometimes, self-loathing comes from dissatisfaction with a trait such as a person's appearance, which leads to doubt and feelings of inadequacy.

However, all human beings have worth and value and the opportunity to nurture self-love.

There are countless signs for self-hatred, and below are listed items that tell survivors they are experiencing self-loathing and not just the occasional negative self-talk.

Focusing on the negative. Instead of focusing on what went right in a conversation, a job at work, or the day people who self-hate concentrate on the bad things that happened and what went wrong.

Not accepting compliments. When someone says something good about the survivor, instead of accepting the compliment, survivors who self-loathe rudely discount what was said and brush them off instead of politely accepting them.

Black and white thinking. Survivors who strongly dislike themselves see themselves as either good or bad with no gray areas in between. When these self-hating survivors make an error, they feel like everything is ruined and that they are a failure.

Taking criticism as a personal attack. Criticism is the best way to improve one's ability to complete a task, yet survivors who self-hate take it as a personal attack and brood over it long after.

Misplaced beliefs about feelings. Survivors who self-loathe take their emotions and feelings as fact, assuming how they feel must reflect the truth. When the survivor feels like a failure, they believe they are indeed a failure instead of allowing the feeling to fade.

Have a pity party. Survivors who self-loathe have pity parties for themselves, feeling they have been given a raw deal in life or that everything in life is against their ability to succeed.

Pushing away people. Self-loathing individuals push away partners and friends, fearing that it will end badly when someone gets too close.

Are afraid to dream. Self-hating survivors of complex trauma are afraid to aspire and dream because they feel they need to live in a protective bubble of their own making. They may also be afraid of failure or success, looking down on themselves no matter what they do.

Believing that other people are selfish and dishonest. The viewpoint of some survivors of their world is very cynical. They feel that people with a positive outlook on life are naïve or lying. These folks have a very bleak outlook on their lives and the world.

Trouble letting go of mistakes. When survivors who hate themselves are confronted by a mistake they have made, they cannot forgive themselves and move on. They may ruminate upon past failures, which hold them back from growth.

Feel like an outsider. Self-hating survivors find they always feel like an outsider and are constantly attempting to fit in. They may feel that other people dislike them and cannot understand why anyone would want to spend time with them.

Although there are many traits to someone who strongly dislikes themselves, one can do things to help end, or at least ease, the self-loathing process.

One way is to talk back to your inner critic. The inner critic in each of us can bring encouragement and self-compassion that aids us in recognizing where we have done wrong and what is needed to make a mistake right.

However, an inner critic that criticizes, judges, or demeans us whether or not the criticism is deserved can destroy a person's emotional well-being, destroy self-esteem, and cause self-loathing. Talking back to the inner critic and establishing an ally with the inner nurturer, that part of a survivor that is protective and encouraging, one can overcome the voice that tells one that they are a loser.

Saying positive affirmations to oneself every day, preferably several times a day, can silence the inner critic and bring it under control.

Another practice that will help survivors move toward self-love is to practice self-compassion. Self-compassion means looking at situations differently by seeing all the good things the survivor has accomplished and ending their trait to have black and white thinking.

The survivor can start small by thinking of one thing they have done that was good and one thing that is good that has occurred or that they did. With the wrong thing, did the world come to an end?

If it didn't, and of course it did not, then they can question why they are catastrophizing the event. Then survivors need to look with open eyes at the good things they have and allow themselves to enjoy and savor the fact that they accomplished it. This behavior will open them up to more positive feelings about themselves and allow self-love to develop.

Yet, a third way to move away from self-loathing is to spend time with positive people. Instead of being with people who make them feel bad about themselves, survivors need to spend more time with positive people who make them feel good.

Hanging out with positive people will rub off on a survivor, leading them to realize good feelings about themselves, leading them to where the self-hate will end.

A fourth method for learning to end self-loathing is to move towards the life you want by taking small baby steps to find the career path you want, getting out of debt, or ending or finding a relationship you desire. First, survivors need to determine their values and start behaving toward them as once they have, they will find it easier to feel confident and move on.

The fifth suggestion to healing self-loathing is to seek and see a therapist. If a survivor has DID especially, they will want to seek a trauma-informed therapist or have experience dealing with dissociative identity disorder. A good therapist can aid in healing the wounds that have caused self-hatred and teach one how to learn to love themselves.

Self-Love

Many victims of severe and repeated childhood abuse were never taught self-acceptance or to love themselves. This is such a tragedy as people who live with dissociative identity disorder and survivors who do not are some of the kindest and most selfless on the planet.

Learning how to exhibit earnest self-love takes some learning and unlearning at the same time. However, self-love is a powerful state to teach to oneself, as it is the catalyst for physical, psychological, and spiritual growth. The more one exhibits self-love, the more they can attract people and events that will support their well-being.

One cannot get self-love by changing their appearance or getting a better job. One also cannot get self-love by having a relationship. Even the most wonderful and beautiful relationship will fail if one does not have a sense of self-love. I'm not speaking of self-absorption where the person thinks only of and cares about themselves. I'm speaking of an inner love that accepts who we are with all our flaws.

Neither is self-love isn't only a state of feeling good. Instead, self-love is a state of appreciation for oneself that grows from actions that support us and allows us to grow as individuals while loving and caring for others. Self-love is energetic and grows through us to help us mature.

With self-love, we grow more patient and kind with ourselves while recognizing our weaknesses and strengths. Because of self-love, we are more compassionate for ourselves and help us recognize our personal meaning.

Methods to Cultivate Self-Love

While each of us must find our own way to self-love, there are five methods one might find helpful in cultivating it.

1. **Seek what you need instead of what you want**. In seeking your needs and finding answers for them instead of being caught up in all the wants that dangle before you one can find a lasting love for themselves. In turning away something that feels good and exciting and instead of what you need, you can move forward with your life. By focusing on what you need, you turn away from behavior that is automatic and get you into trouble and keep you stuck in the past and decrease self-acceptance and self-love.

2. **Be mindful**. To cultivate self-love, one needs to know what they think, feel, and want. By practicing mindfulness, one can maintain a healthy sense of self and act on that knowledge. One becomes self-sufficient in their love for themselves instead of dependent on someone else doing it.

3. **Set healthy boundaries.** By setting firm boundaries and maintaining them, we set

limits and tell others where they may and may not tread. Because of these boundaries, you will love life and have a spiritual and emotional awakening.

4. **Forgive yourself.** People are the hardest on themselves. However, being hard on oneself has the downside of taking responsibility for their actions and punishing themselves for mistakes or a failure to grow.

One must accept that they are only human before you can love yourself. Try to remember there are no failures in life so long as you try. Accept that you will be okay when you inevitably fail. Failure is a simple fact of life. Everyone fails, but those who move on to self-love learn that they learn from their failures and are not destroyed by them.

5. **Live purposefully.** If one lives with purpose, they will learn to accept and love themselves more, no matter where they are in life. One's purpose does not need to be clear as water to you. If you intend to live life to the fullest and feel good about yourself when you succeed, you will find

you love yourself. Establish your living intentions and learn to live up to them.

Loving yourself is the most important step towards healing you can make, and it will change your life forever. Self-love will also set you up for acceptance and the eventual integration of child alters.

Child Alters: A Blast from the Past

Trauma-Time

Like all alters in a DID system, child alters are pieces of the survivor stuck in what is called trauma-time.

Trauma-time is a strange phenomenon experienced by survivors of all genders and other demographic descriptions. Trauma-time occurs because traumatic memories are stored in a unique form than other memories. Traumatic memories seem to become encapsulated and unmetabolized in the limbic (emotional region) of the brain, where time means nothing.

This compartmentalizing of memories is vital to helping a child who is being abused to cope and survive.

When a child is experiencing frightening or threatening events where there is a good chance they will live in an unsafe environment, how do survivors cope and survive in such a world?

The child does it by remaining vigilant and reacting swiftly to suspicious input from the senses, putting them in the position of not caring about the passing of time. Time becomes fluid and means little in such an environment.

Adult survivors remain hypervigilant and ready for trouble, not understanding time as others do. This statement is accurate, even though the original trauma may have occurred decades before.

Just because the survivor has grown older and beyond the reach of their childhood abusers means nothing to the limbic brain, which comprises the amygdala, our first line of defense against trauma, and the hippocampus, the organ in the brain responsible for memory consolidation.

The limbic brain is designed without an internal clock and is forever vigilant, watching for trouble in our environment.

No matter how many times the survivor has suffered at the hands of their abusers, a sound, smell, or other sense may remind the limbic system of the danger once faced triggering the limbic system to cause a surge of cortisol in the brain. The cortisol causes the heart to race, palms to sweat, and thinking to become disorganized and fragmented.

Many trauma survivors dissociate, meaning that the thinking self becomes separated from the emotional self that holds all the memories of past trauma. Suddenly, after a trigger, the survivor responds as they did years earlier. Flashbacks may occur with the reliving of the event. Emotional flashbacks may also occur, dragging with them all the emotions felt in the past when there was real danger.

The survivor, in this scenario, has become trapped in trauma-time, lost in the horrific events of the past as though they were happening today.

Often, survivors feel confused, and as others around them witness their extreme behaviors, they are later exposed to the double whammy of feeling guilt and shame.

During trauma-time, survivors operate from an emotional self that holds the feelings related to the trauma and can cause one to lose track of everything in the present, including what year it is, where they are, and that they are not in danger now.

It may take seconds or hours to regain knowledge of where they are and what time it is in the now.

Trauma-time leaves a multiple survivor reliving the abuse or reacting to today's environment as though it were years earlier when they were small and vulnerable.

One way to defeat trauma-time is to practice staying centered, tolerant of stress, and self-aware. These skills don't happen overnight or by osmosis; one must practice them before and during an attack of trauma-time

Ending the intrusion of traumatic memories and child alters involves breaking the silence of child abuse and telling someone else what happened. Too often, the voices of the inner children that exist inside a survivor are silenced for fear of retribution or losing control. However, ignoring the small voices crying inside your mind is cruel to you and will keep you ill.
The therapist's office is a safe place to bring survivors stuck in trauma-time into the

present. Therapy allows one to integrate the memories with helpful information, like the fact that they are no longer in danger and that the survivors are now adults who have rights and choices. Talking in therapy to a therapist allows one to view the memories of what happened differently and reconnect a survivor to their emotions.

The Concept of the Inner Child

We now recognize that all humans have inner children, but at one time, that fact remained a mystery. Then, Carl Jung, a protégé of Sigmund Freud, became interested in what he called the 'child inside.' Jung became aware that he had lost his interest in creativity and his childhood love of building things. Jung realized the emotions that arose when remembering his childhood love of building and formed a relationship with the 'small boy inside him.'

By the 70s, the concept of an inner child was accepted widely and helped to form the basis of many 12-step movements.

Today, inner child work is the basis for many therapists work with clients who were traumatized in childhood.

For survivors, finding that part of themselves that has been caught in trauma-time is both beneficial and terrifying.

It is beneficial to multiples because working with their inner children allows them to regain their emotions and put the memories of what happened in the past where they belong.

It is terrifying to multiples because the memories held by their inner child-selves hold all the emotions they pushed back and tried to forget to survive.

Unresolved memories and emotions can interrupt the flow of a survivor's life, leaving them wallowing in fear and frustration.

Also, unresolved issues can cause disability and lost relationships.

Inner child work includes the ability to contact the inner child living inside the survivor and working to connect the feelings they have to their emotions. Working with inner children allows multiples to see where issues faced in adulthood originate.

Inner child work can help you discover:

- Emotions that need to be released that are keeping you from finding your full potential

- How to recognize and meet unmet needs
- Unhelpful childlike behavior patterns
- How to increase self-care
- How to increase one's self-respect
- How to increase one's self-esteem

Working with one's inner child is difficult, especially for multiples who harbor in their minds unspeakable memories of severe childhood abuse.

The Benefits of Knowing Your Inner Child

While multiples learning to understand their inner children is daunting, there are many benefits to acknowledging their existence and that what they remember is valid.

These benefits may include:

Increased Playfulness. One might find themselves feeling free of the constraints of being an adult, even if for only a short while. The relaxation playing brings to us is immeasurable in its benefits to our mental and physical health.

New Confidence. Upon contact with your inner child, you may feel the confidence you once knew to try new things and to go on adventures. This awakening of the adventurous confidence in you will make persistence much more enjoyable and help you reach your adult goals.

Better Physical Health. Children and adults benefit from having a sense of belonging and community. Their immune systems are bolstered when we get to know ourselves better, and because of that, relate better to the world.

A Better Understanding of Yourself.

A Better Understanding of Yourself. Through accessing repressed memories and emotions, you can discover what is causing you to have problems in your adult life.

Feeling Self-Compassion. Self-love is so foreign to some people that they reject the notion outright. The idea of telling themselves that they love them is abhorrent to them. Through contacting the inner child, one can learn to love that child inside and learn to love and accept every part of their self.

Learn Self-Care. While getting to know one's inner child, it is impossible not to feel a need to care for them. We might even feel protective and the need to mother them. In the process, one is learning to care about oneself and how to take care of your needs.

Getting to know one's inner children may seem frightening, especially since they hold such powerful emotions that are tied to highly traumatic events. However, there are enormous healing benefits.

Recognizing Your Wounded Inner Child

When you were a child, you, like all children, deserved to feel safe from harm, fear, and lack. You deserved to feel safety physically, emotionally, and spiritually. When children feel safe with the families they were born into, their boundaries are respected, and their needs are being met.

In childhood trauma, a survivor's childhood is full of unmet needs, and this destroys a child's sense of safety. Then in adulthood, these inner children never go away and neither does the feelings of being unsafe.

When children feel continuously endangered, a massive wound opens in their psyche that is so painful that many adults unknowingly repress all memory of them (Kneisl, 1991).

It is critical to remember that words can hurt as severely as actions with some voices of their abusers echoing in the mind of the survivor, leaving deep scars that last a lifetime.

These words consist of negative behaviors
by perpetrators including:

- Not allowing a child to have their own
  opinions
- Discouragement from playing or
  having fun
- Not allowed to display powerful
  emotions
- Punishing for speaking up
- Continuously shaming by caregivers
- Not allowing spontaneity
- Was not given appropriate hugs,
  kisses, or cuddles

Children who do not receive the emotional
and physical support they need to grow up to
become hurting adults.

Getting to know the inner children of a DID
system if vital and acknowledging their
wounds is critical, as the harm done to the
inner children is directly correlated with the
ways you feel unsafe as an adult.

Here are some signs that you have internal
wounded children:

- You feel that there is something wrong with you
- You are a people-pleaser
- You are a rebel and feel alive when in conflict with someone else
- You might be a hoarder
- You cannot let go of possessions and people
- You experience anxiety about something new
- You feel guilty for setting boundaries
- You feel driven to be a super-achiever
- You are ridged and a perfectionist
- You having problems starting and finishing tasks
- You may exhibit constant self-criticism
- You feel ashamed for expressing emotions
- You feel ashamed of your body
- You have a deep distrust of anyone else
- You avoid conflict, no matter what the cost,
- You have a fear of abandonment

If you recognize yourself in many, if not all, these signs, you have wounded children living inside you.

The Wounds of Neglect Experienced by Inner Children

To understand how to overcome childhood trauma, one must first know what child abuse is. Child trauma isn't only physical, emotional, sexual, and narcissistic abuse, it also involves neglect.

Children crave and deserve to have their needs met and to feel safe and loved. Unfortunately, many children in our society today are neglected.

It is critical to understand what childhood neglect is about. There are three types of childhood neglect, physical, emotional, and psychological.

Physical Neglect. Physical safety and nourishment are basic human needs that are to be given freely by caregivers to children. However, in physical neglect, these rights are violated and are lacking. Unfortunately, physical neglect does not mean only that the child was kept from food and shelter.

It also means several forms of abuse are taking place, such as sexual abuse.

The results of neglect are devastating.
Below are only a few of the negative affects
physical neglect has on children and the
adults they become.

- Low self-esteem
- Eating disorders
- Self-harm
- Addictions
- Violent behavior
- Sexual dysfunction

Emotional Neglect. In this type of neglect,
a child's caregiver did not show enough
interest in the child's emotional needs for
support, respect, and love. In these cases,
either the caregiver ignores or condemns any
emotional expressions that the child might
need.

Like with physical abuse, the symptoms and
outcomes of this type of neglect are dire in
adulthood.

- Low self-worth
- Repressing emotions
- Ignoring one's own emotional needs
- Depression

- Anxiety
- Shunning Emotional closeness or intimacy

Psychological Neglect. This kind of neglect occurred when the child's caregivers failed to listen, nurture, and embrace the beautiful human beings that they are. This form of neglect includes any or all:

- Name-calling
- Insults
- Ridicule
- Yelling
- Gaslighting
- Lack of privacy
- Making overt threats

The symptoms that occur when the inner child endures this type of neglect and inhabit adults can be:

- Deep-seated feelings of anger
- Inability to love themselves
- The development of low self-esteem
- Addictions
- Neuroses
- Psychological illnesses

- Physical illnesses
- Showing a lack of respect for others
- Problems with sustaining a healthy relationship

The wounds children incur become the wounded inner children of adults who have grown up and later have left that home.

What are Child Alters?

Dissociative identity disorder, previously known as multiple personality disorder, is characterized by more than one sense of identity or sense of self. These altered states of sense of self are known as alters, parts, or people in a system.

What are alters? Why are many altars in a DID system children?

A survivor who forms alters does so to protect themselves against the ravages of the emotions and pain associated with severe child abuse. Since much of the pain, sorrow, and fear occurred to survivors when they were small children, it only makes sense that many of the alters in their system would be children.

Alters can take control of a survivor's body, although they are all parts of the same person. Each alter can function independently, which is where most of the chaos experienced by survivors comes from.

Altars form because of prolonged childhood trauma starting before the age of nine. It is nearly impossible for a person to form alternate states of self after that age. Sometimes alters are incorrectly called ego states or alternate egos, but those states exist in all people regardless of childhood trauma and do not involve dissociative symptoms such as amnesia.

Alters may have different ages, genders, sexual preferences, and personal likes. Some alters have names while some will not. Alters may take on different roles or functions related to daily life, different attitudes, and different preferences.

Some alters in a DID system will remember the distress and trauma from the past, while others are completely amnesiac for them.

Child alters are less likely to front the body than older ones, but they can and will surface under the right circumstances. When child alters do surface, they are who they seem to be, innocent children who need adult supervision. Child alters are in danger of being victimized because they do not see the world from an adult's perspective. Instead, they think, act, and have age

appropriate knowledge as an outside child
would.

Trauma Time

Survivors of severe abuse and neglect in childhood often live with the phenomenon known as trauma time.

Trauma time occurs when traumatic memories are condensed and then stored in the limbic system (the emotional region of the brain). The limbic part of the brain is the most primitive region, and its function is to digest and make sense of sensory input from the environment around the survivor. The limbic system does not recognize time; indeed, in the limbic system, time has no meaning.

This region of our brain helped us to survive as a species.

Some trauma survivors use dissociation as a defense mechanism to handle the intense emotions associated with trauma time. This defense mechanism is fine and dandy so long as we do not become so dissociated from ourselves and our emotions that they become separated from us.

The limbic region of the brain is always on the alert for danger and, when triggered, causes a cascading effect on our brain and body, setting us up for the fight/flight/freeze response. Suddenly, survivors find themselves reacting to a sight, smell, or sound and are thrown back years or even decades into the past where they experienced abuse or neglect.

During the trauma response to trauma time, one may 'forget' they are adults and a child alter may emerge. Mostly, child alters will not come out if the child does not feel completely safe and switching into one does not mean there are spectacular changes in the survivor's behavior.

However, some people experience the emergence of a child alter into public life, but this is rare. Instead, the survivor may see the traumatic memory through the eyes of a child alter and forget temporarily who they are, where they are, and even what their name is.

Once the limbic system is triggered, the survivor will experience the effects of increased cortisol levels, such as a racing heart, sweaty palms, and disorganized plus fragmented thoughts.

Because the survivor, now devolved into a child alter, is terrified they may strike out at those around them exhibiting anger which they will later regret and feel shame.

It is critical to remember that you are responsible for everything you do and say even while dissociated into a child alter. That the child alter is you and you are them is vital to keep in mind. It is also important to remember that for all intents and purposes, when you are dissociated into a child alter you are for all intents and purposes a child. You are not just pretending to be a child; you are a child.

Keeping in mind that child alters are children, it is critical to set firm boundaries with them and rules that they can follow. For one, a child alter should never get behind the steering wheel of a car. Set a firm rule that they may not do so and most likely the child alter will follow your rules because they desperately need them.

Child alters lost in trauma time need reassurance, love, and understanding to help them come to live in the present 'now' where everything is better. Invite your child alters to leave trauma time and show them how much you love and care for them as this is the most important step of healing.

ANPs and EPs

All alters in a system, including child alters, can be broadly classed as either apparently normal parts (ANPs) or emotional parts (EPs). In addition, some alters may have one or more type or role. People who are enormously fragmented may have many parts comprising many, many child alters stuck in trauma-time.

Survivors who have over 100 parts and involve dozens of members or systems that have lots of subsystems.

Apparently normal parts, previously called the host personality, are identified as the alter who manages day-to-day life and rarely hold or remember trauma memories before brain maturity. There can be over one ANP each with different roles to play to keep the person alive and functioning. An ANP may be disconnected emotionally or amnesiac to past traumatic events.

Emotional parts are pieces of the same personality that hold traumatic memories and are stuck in trauma-time, especially in the sensory aspects of the memory. These parts include child alters are unaware of passaging time.

Some EPs are nor emotional at all and some may not even be human.

While alters come in all shapes, sizes, ages, and purpose, below are a few of the alters that can occur inside a multiple.

Persecutor. These alters have taken on the role modeled for them by their abuser(s). Persecutors may have taken on different aspects and behaviors of a past abuser.

Infant alters. These child alters are pre-verbal and remain the same age or they can grow and take on different roles in the system.

Caretaker alters. These alters are protectors and manage the care of the other alters in a DID system by being motherly towards the others. Often, caretaker alters lack awareness of their self-care and become exhausted. These alters have a limited ability to socialize, play, or explore their world.

Child alters. Littles the multiple stuck in trauma-time and the topic of this book. Child alters hold memories of the abuse, and some have the speech or appearance of a very young child.

Child alters are highly protected by the caretaker and core alters in the system as they are very vulnerable to attack. Some child alters are fun-loving, holding only positive memories while others are fearful remembering only the trauma that caused them to form.

Sometimes child alters fantasize are obsessed with being the perfect child and having come from the perfect family.

Core/Original alters. The original or apparently normal part of the personality of a survivor.

Dormant alters. These alters have chosen, for whatever reason, to "go to sleep" or become inactive. Sometimes this occurs because the trauma they held has been resolved. Dormant alters are dormant because the right amount of stress can trigger them back to life.

Fragments. Some alters may only hold brief glimpses of the trauma incurred in childhood and thus have a smaller number of emotions. Fragments may have a range of emotions, but they are more subtle and rarely do fragments front. A fragment may have a special purpose, such as holding anger, rage, or sadness.

Gatekeeper. This type of alter has the unenviable job of keeping other alters stuck in trauma-time from appearing. Gatekeepers may also hold and control, which alters can take control of the body and which cannot.

Host. The presenting part of a DID system, an apparently normal part, is known as the host and they have executive control over the body most of the time. A survivor living with DID will have over one host throughout their lifetime.

Child alters can be any type of alter, but mainly they inhabit the world of the emotional part, holding specific memories of something that happened to the survivor long ago.

There are many more types of alters.

How Do Child Alters Form?

Alters in a DID system are formed before the age of five (by some nine) because of severe, repeated, and traumatic child abuse.

Alters of any form manage overwhelming trauma or changes in everyday life that are stressful and cannot be managed by the existing personality. Child alters are formed to keep the memories and emotions of what happened far away from the host so that the child can continue to live without going insane.

It is vital to remember that some survivors remember partial or entire events of trauma from when they were children, but the existence of child alters makes recalling these traumatic events difficult.

The culture in which the child lives directly affects the creation of alters. Religious beliefs of the survivor's parents may insinuate that the alters are demons or some other form of spiritual creature.

Alters, especially child alters, are neither good nor bad. They exist to protect survivors from the horrors of the past.

In adulthood, alters can be created if the person already has dissociative identity disorder in response to stress or triggers that are too hard for the existing alter system to handle.

Some people experience the formation of alters because of ritual abuse performed by an organized perpetrator group. In these groups, children are harmed and sometimes alters are intentionally formed in the children they abuse to train them for a specific job.

It is critical to understand that alters are formed in early childhood long before the brain has moved on into middle childhood. The brain goes through stages of pruning away any circuits (synapses) that it rules unneeded and one of these occurs around the ages of 5-9, thus cutting off any possibility of forming alters unless the child has already done so.

Thus, although it is impossible to say never, adults do not and cannot form alters like exist in a dissociative identity disorder system.

Child alters are innocent parts of a survivor caught up in trauma-time as fragments or entire entities.

All alters are made of one person.

Healing Child Alters

Inner Child Work

All children deserve to feel safe—safe from harm, fear, and lack. Safety does not mean only physical security but also emotional and spiritual well-being as well. When children feel safe within the families they were born into, their boundaries are respected, and they their needs are met and secure.

Childhood trauma, where the child's needs are not met, destroys a child's sense of safety, causing them to become hypervigilant and scared. In adulthood, these inner children never go away, and neither do their feelings of being unsafe and that the world is a horrible and dangerous place. When a child feels continually endangered, a massive gaping wound opens in their psyche that is so painful that many adults unknowingly repress it. (Kneisl 1991)

Words can hurt as severely as actions with some signals given to children, leaving deep scars that can last a lifetime. Some of these statements and actions made by parents that leave open wounds are as follows.

- Not allowing a child to have their own opinions
- Discouragement from playing or having fun
- Not allowed to display powerful emotions
- Punishing for speaking up
- Continuously shaming by caregivers
- Not allowing spontaneity
- Was not given appropriate hugs, kisses, or cuddles

Children who do not receive emotional and physical support grow up to be hurting adults with some forming dissociative identity disorder.

The concept of the inner child began with Carl Jung, who became interested in the 'child inside' after he broke with Sigmund Freud to form his own practice. Jung knew he had lost his interest in creativity and his childhood love of building things. Jung also realized the emotions that arose when he remembered his childhood love of building and formed a relationship with the 'small boy inside him.'

By the 1970s, the concept of the inner child was being used widely. It helped to form the basis of many 12-step and codependency movements. Today, inner child work is at the base of most work therapists do with their clients who were traumatized as children and those who have formed DID.

All human beings have a part of themselves that has never grown up. That part may feel and react to their circumstances, like a child. This enigmatic piece of our psyche is called the inner child.

Finding that part of oneself that may or may not be caught in trauma-time can be both beneficial and terrifying. If one's inner child is happy and healthy, then he or she will cause you to experience joy at the little things. If, however, the inner child was traumatized, such as in the abuse that was endured by those with DID, one might find their inner child acting out and having tantrums.

As one might suspect, an inner child that is misbehaving because of unresolved trauma will interrupt relationships and one's life.

Inner child work includes the ability to contact the inner children in your dissociated system and working to connect with their feelings and emotions. Inner child work allows one to see where issues one may face in adulthood came from.

Inner child work can help you discover:

- Emotions that need to be released that are keeping you from finding your full potential
- How to recognize and meet unmet needs
- Unhelpful childlike behavior patterns
- How to increase self-care
- How to increase one's self-respect
- How to increase one's self-esteem

Inner children that live in your psyche directly influence all that you do. As adult survivors, we are covertly and sometimes overtly, controlled by our subconscious inner child, and this leaves a child in charge of their lives. When wounded, these little are full of anger, shame, and sometimes rage because of the maltreatment they endured.

Inner children are the lens through which we, as injured adults, make our decisions.

Can you imagine your children or a child you see on the street trying to make sense of adult relationships? Or make career decisions? Predictably, such attempts could only end in disaster. However, this happens every day in the lives of people who have a wounded inner child.

These small, lost, and lonely parts of ourselves are afraid and insecure, and that can make our lives miserable. However, there is hope. Inner child work, including self-parenting, can ease the pain and heal the wounds left behind by caregivers who were abusive and toxic.

Beginning the Healing Journey:
Understanding Psychological Trauma

One cannot discuss healing alters without first talking about without talking about psychological trauma. The Diagnostic and Statistical Manual of Mental Disorders (DSM) defines psychological trauma as:

"The direct personal experience of an event that involves actual or threatened death or serious injury; threat to one's physical integrity, witnessing an event that involves the above experience, learning about unexpected or violent death, serious harm, or threat of death, or injury experienced by a family member or close associate. Memories associated with trauma are implicit, pre-verbal, and cannot be recalled, but can be triggered by stimuli from the in vivo (within the living person's) environment. The person's response to aversive details of traumatic event involve intense fear, helplessness, or horror. In children, it is manifested as disorganized or agitative behaviors."

As you can see, this definition is very broad. There are several key elements worthy of mentioning; however, "the person sees or fears death or severe injury and a threat to their body."

Also, please note that they have listed as a response to these emotionally stimulating events: intense fear, helplessness, or horror.

A person who has been traumatized may experience many of the following psychological and physical symptoms:

- Shock, denial, or disbelief
- Confusion, difficulty concentrating
- Anger, irritability, mood swings
- Anxiety and fear
- Guilt, shame, self-blame
- Withdrawing from others
- Feeling sad or hopeless
- Feeling disconnected or numb
- Insomnia or nightmares
- Fatigue
- Being startled easily
- Racing heartbeat
- Edginess and agitation
- Aches and pains

- Muscle tension
- Childhood trauma forever changes who children are as they grow into adulthood, and as we shall see further on, changes us physically as well

Brain Changes Brought on by Psychological Trauma

The chemicals that we make in response to stress are important to our being able to escape or confront danger. However, when the developing brain of a young child is bathed in stress hormones and never returns to normal levels, the results can be disastrous. Such is the case in children who live in traumatic environments where they are in constant danger physically, emotionally, or sexually.

What hasn't been discussed is the fact that the brain is divided into two hemispheres or halves, right and left, each responsible for the separate ways we store the information we receive from three varied parts of our thinking brain.

The primary functions of the left hemisphere include language, math, and logic. The right side regulates our ability to determine special differences in our environment, face recognition, visual imagery, and music. These functions are settled forever. Rather, we can reroute what we need to when one side becomes damaged. This been observed in people who have brain injuries from accidents, disease, and stroke.

During the development of a child's brain from birth to around five years, extensive changes to the size of the brain and the number of neurons with their connectedness occur.

Myelination. We create myelin to increase the size of the brain by creating layers around brain cells, and this increases the speed of information that can be processed.

Neurons (brain cells) connect to each other and communicate, and this connectedness depends on our childhood experiences. We start out at birth with many more brain cells than we need and prune them once new connections are established.

These changes that occur in the brain during development are called neural plasticity, and this nature decreases. An interesting and important aspect is that the decrease in plasticity over time is different for different systems in the brain. Some areas of the cortex continue to reorganize with experience until late in life, while others, such as language centers, are less likely to change.

Trauma affects this normal development of the brain by interrupting through overstimulation of stress hormones, the ability of the brain to process memory, and the two hemispheres of the brain to communicate. While the survival center (brain stem) continues to keep us alive, the emotional center cannot regulate correctly what memories are stores there, and the hemispheres of the brain become fragmented in their ability to store information. These changes are not reversible.

To fully understand what severe and repeated trauma does to the brains of young children, one must first learn some about the chemicals neurons (brain nerve cells) used to communicate called neurotransmitters and the brain structures most affected by them.

There are many important substances responsible for the activity in our brains, but we shall touch on just a few of these important chemicals and hormones.

Cortisol. Cortisol is a hormone that controls our reactions to stress. This stimulant gives us the energy to fight or flee in the face of danger.

Serotonin and dopamine. These are neurotransmitters that affect our moods and behaviors. These chemicals trigger an increase in heart rate, blood pressure, and reduces blood flow to the gut. It also inhibits the body from releasing bodily wastes such as urine and feces. These responses are important to be ready to face danger.

Norepinephrine and Epinephrine. These neurotransmitters affect mood, behavior, and create the fight/flight/freeze response. This chemical mobilizes the brain and body for action by stimulating the areas of the body needed to fight or flee. It raises awareness, alertness, and vigilance. It also enhances the formation and retrieval of memory, focuses attention, increases restlessness and anxiety. **Glutamate**. Glutamate is a neurotransmitter that excites nerve cells. In balance, it is required to organize our perception of our experiences.

Under normal circumstances, these chemicals allow us to move about in our environment very well. However, when young children experience repeated and extreme traumatic events, the production of these chemicals is altered. Levels of cortisol are decreased, norepinephrine and epinephrine are elevated, and serotonin decreases.

Prolonged exposure, such as in repeated and severe childhood trauma, can have dire consequences. There can be behavioral changes, such as depression, fear, and lack of impulse control. Also, there can be an impaired perception of reality and changed the filing of memories.

Because of the existence of severe and repeated trauma, the imbalance of these chemicals interferes with the storage of declarative memories, so the child may not remember what happened, or if they do they do not remember correctly. The sizes of the parts of the brain can be altered by continual bathing in the above substances, causing lifelong changes that can alter the future of the traumatized child's life.

The constant submersion of a child's brain in stress hormones can change a child's brain and its ability to function forever.

One researcher, Martin Teicher, has found evidence of how a person's brain is affected by childhood trauma. In 1993, he found brain abnormalities in 54% of children with histories of physical abuse, but only 27% in children who had no history of abuse. The numbers jump alarmingly when measuring children who have been sexually abused. The research showed 72% of children with histories of this type of abuse with abnormal brains. (Teicher, 1993). The regions found to be most affected by trauma, not only in Teicher's work but in subsequent research, are:

- **The Hippocampus.** This part of our brains handles declarative memory, emotions, and critical for learning. It allows us to process memories and manage the emotions that go along with them. Research has found a reduction in the size of the hippocampi of adults who were severely traumatized as children of 19%.

- **The Amygdala**. This structure handles the unconscious storage and processing of emotions and starting the flight/fight/freeze response. The amygdalae of adults who were exposed to extreme and repeated trauma as children are often hypersensitive to the information received through the senses and can trigger a strong fear response even when there is currently no danger present.

Through the years since Dr. Teicher first found that a child's brain development can be severely curtailed by trauma, there has been much research and many papers written that back up his assumptions and findings.

The hippocampus and amygdala work together to form a cohesive memory of events. When there is extreme and repeated trauma in childhood, this communication is disrupted. Memories can either be enhanced or totally repressed, depending on the way these two vital parts of the brain interact.

There are many effects caused by this disruption of communication. One is the dysregulation of emotions.

Since the amygdala senses danger when there is none, the hippocampus is hard-pressed to respond appropriately.

Many times, child alters will respond to stimuli today as if it were a repeat of the trauma they lived through in the past.

Temper tantrums and crying spells are caused by the continual bombardment of the amygdala. Because these two structures are diminished in size, depression, anxiety, and irritability are often seen.

Working with Child Alters

While working with inner children may sound easy, it is not. Because it is so difficult, it is highly recommended that inner child work only occurs in the presence of a trained mental health professional.

Try to find a therapist who is trauma-informed or has experience treating dissociative disorders. This is a tall order, as on average therapists and even psychiatrists receive only three to six weeks of training about how to treat dissociative disorders, let alone dissociative identity disorder.

However, once you have found a therapist, you will find that the first thing you must do is to open a dialogue with your child alters (or any alters.)

To get to know the parts of yourself who are all stuck in trauma-time better, it may be necessary to form a safe place in your mind. It can be a warm, sandy beach, a sunny flower-strewn meadow, or the top of a mountain. Whatever works for you and your system is what you need to choose.

There are several reasons for forming this safe place:

- It helps all your parts feel safe
- It allows a place to go when you feel overwhelmed
- It allows a place where you can hold conversations with each other

A survivor's safe place is vital to overcoming the hesitancy of the alters who have spent a lifetime hiding away from them. The emotions and memories they harbor have been hidden away from the waking self and alters will be highly reluctant to sharing them.

Not only this, but alters, especially child alters, may feel put upon by a request to come out and introduce themselves, There may even be resistance from older alters bordering on defiance because they feel frightened at the prospect of their memories and emotions being in danger of not belonging solely to them anymore.

It is vital to understand that words are mighty things. Words can build up and tear down. Words can affirm or destroy. Words are a potent force for good or for evil. Understanding these facts will help you know what you should and should not say to your alters, who are all you.

To begin a discussion with inner parts, first, make sure you are safe. This type of dialogue may require you to be in the presence of a mental health professional, at least at first, until you feel more connected and grounded.

Remember this too. If an alter is a child, they should be treated as children. Do not talk about huge grown-up topics; instead, meet them where they are and allow yourself to feel their emotions. Always keep in mind that alters may refuse to meet you in your safe place. But, even if they refuse, eventually they will come if you give them a reason to want to.

Once grounded, opening your talk with some simple questions asked inside your safe place of your alters. Questions can be as simple as "What's your name?" or "How old are you?" Do not expect an answer right at

First, because you have most likely been afraid of your alters before this day; they may also be fearful of you.

Some other useful hints for starting an inner dialogue with alters are:

Welcome Them. Make the first move and take an interest in the alter you are speaking with. Allow them to acclimate to being with you and set them at ease as much as you can. You can also tell them how excited you are to be meeting your alters and show our enthusiasm and excitement.

Set Boundaries and Rules. One of the best things about starting an inner dialogue is that rules and boundaries can be set to assure that your life becomes more manageable. Rules such as no one in your system can overwhelm you with flashbacks in your safe place, and boundaries such as no cussing (or whatever you wish) are essential. Children need and love rules, and so do many adults, thus making some for your safe place makes perfect sense.

Use Their Name. Say their name often to establish that you are listening and validating what they are saying. Obviously, this hint only works if you know the alters name.

Offer to Help. Your inner parts are there because something horrid happened to you in childhood. They hold all the memories and secrets of what occurred and are in pain. If you offer your inner parts help, such as telling them you are going to protect them now, they will grow in trust as time goes by.

Listen. By listening more than you speak, you will learn much from your alters. They will let you in on their hopes and dreams, which, of course, are what you wanted when you were their age.

Feel. Feel the emotions from needs that were not met in your childhood. It is okay to weep over what was torn from you in the past.

Re-parenting Oneself

Some children live in environments where their parents are unavailable, either physically or emotionally. Sometimes, as with the development of complex post-traumatic stress disorder (CPTSD), children are harmed by those who were supposed to protect and guard them.

In fact, the following quote is valid: "The term Re-parenting designates a therapeutic operation by means the patient is offered new parental figures with positive characteristics" (Del Casale et al. 1982)

These inner children need re-parenting. Adults can't return to their childhood and begin again. So, Re-parenting means giving yourself what you did not receive in childhood from the original parents.

Reparenting involves learning to give your wounded inner child all the love, respect, and dignity they deserved when you were young.

Sometimes survivors dislike the notion that someone else cannot re-parent them. They

balk at the knowledge that no one else can
do the job but themselves.

While it may not be what we adults
want, learning to become our own parent is
the only option to overcome bad parenting
we received in the past.

Children are supposed to learn many life

skills from their parents, including how to

take care of their own emotional and

physical needs. These life skills include:

· Love and Respect
· Self-Belief and Self-Confidence
· Emotional Management
· Excellent Communication Skills

Let's examine together each of these life
skills.

Love and Respect. Parents are supposed to
teach their children to speak to themselves
compassionately. Children need to learn to
respect their values and believes but to be
brave enough to challenge whether or not
they are correct.

Kids need to be taught to respect their
bodies and to set appropriate
boundaries. They also need to know when to
let go of people who do not respect them.
Children also need to learn to value, love,
and respect others, accepting other beliefs
and backgrounds. They need to learn not to
force their beliefs onto others and to express
opinions in a manner that respects other's
feelings.

If any of these skills are missing, the child
grows into an adult who not only does not
love and respect themselves, but also lacks
respect for others.

Self-Belief and Self-Confidence. These two
qualities can only be learned through
experience, and it is up to parents to instill in
their children to have self-belief. This belief
system allows children to have the courage
to take the risks to further themselves in the
world.

Teaching children that there is no such thing
as a failure only opportunities to learn sets
them up to try new things and to accept their
faults. These kids will be more confident
and competent in everything they do.

When parents do not teach their kids self-belief and self-confidence, they allow their children to internalize any mistakes they might make and to wallow in their failures. Children whose parents did not teach them self-belief and self-confidence grow into adults who are afraid to try new things and would rather be a follower rather than a leader.

Emotional Management. Learning to manage one's emotions is one of the most important things a parent can teach their child. Children learn emotional management from watching their parent's example, and if the parent does not regulate their own emotions, the child will not either. The result is adults who are ruled by their emotions and who cannot respond appropriately to emotional stimuli. When faced with feeling depressed or scared, these adults cannot act, and if nothing changes, nothing changes.
These adults become caught in a cycle.

Excellent Communication Skills. The success of adults both professionally and personally relies upon the quality of their communication skills. Parents are to teach their children to use and listen to both verbal and non-verbal communications and respond with authenticity, sensitivity, and actively. When children are not taught to listen to others, they grow up to be adults who are unable to cultivate respectful relationships both at work and at home. Forming deep and lasting relationships becomes extremely difficult when communication skills are compromised by a lack of parenting.

It may seem counterintuitive to think that an adult can be reparented by someone other than their original parents. In fact, many survivors fall into the trap of wanting their original parents to finish the job and hold resentment towards them because they cannot.

At the beginning of treatment, reparenting, a form of transactional analysis occurs when a therapist assumes the role of a new parental figure. The therapist begins to teach their client various life skills that can aid in the child, now an adult, in learning to live productively in the real world.

Reparenting must be carried out carefully by the therapist so that, eventually, the reigns can be turned over to the adult who must then carry on the lessons on their own. To be clear, this is supposed to be what happened initially, but the original parents were too damaged or self-involved to carry out these actions.

After instilling into their client all the lessons they can, the therapist slowly backs off and instead helps the adult to attempt by trial and error to live successfully.

The therapist needs to be vigilant that their client does not become entirely dependent on them. The idea is for the adult to grow into their own parent, not for the therapist to become a forever parent to their client.

Forms of Reparenting

While Re-parenting sounds straightforward, there are several methods and forms of carrying out this form of psychotherapy.

- Total Regression
- Time-Limited Regression
- Spot Reparenting
- Self-Reparenting

Below, we shall look at each one. It is critical to remember that therapists sometimes employ over one method of Re-parenting.

Total Regression. First developed by Jacqui Lee Schiff, this type of Re-parenting was derived from transactional analysis theory. Transactional analysis theory suggests that social transactions can be analyzed to determine the state of the communicator as parent-like, childlike, or adult-like based on their behavior.

The survivor lives with the therapist for several years in an institution setting, during which they are cared for and nurtured by their therapist. The therapist offers all the care and nurturing the survivor needs with the goal of totally changing the client's parent ego state (Schiff 1977).

Obviously, this form of Re-parenting technique is seldom if ever used in the United States.

Time-Limited Regression. Developed by Thomas Wilson, time-limited Re-parenting is used to treat patients who live with the diagnosis of schizophrenia.

The client is required to attend five two-hour sessions with the therapist instead of living with them. During this time, nurturing is offered that is more intense and more structured than total regression Re-parenting (Moroney 1985).

While this form of Re-parenting is primarily used with people who have schizophrenia, it can also be helpful for those who have DID.

Spot Reparenting. This form of Re-parenting was developed by Russell Osnes and involves less time-intensity than regression therapy. This form of Re-parenting focuses on survivors traumatized by specific traumas and incidences rather than just on general disturbances in childhood (Osnes 1974).

Self-Reparenting. This form of self-parenting is the most popular of the Re-parenting methods used today. Self-Re-parenting was developed by Muriel James and involved not replacing the parent ego state but confirming the positive aspects already present in the survivor's ego. Instead of the therapy being reliant on the therapist being the parent, instead, the survivor is the primary agent (James 1998).

This form of self-parenting is incredibly powerful as it allows the person to learn from the therapist but to be their own agent in their recovery. Thus, they learn to love, respect, and care about themselves the way they should have been taught by their parents of origin.

There is no substitute for good parenting. However, if you did not receive what you needed in childhood, it is never too late to begin anew by Re-parenting yourself.

Reparenting yourself allows you to give yourself all the love, respect, and dignity you did not receive in childhood. As your own parent, you can spend your time enjoying your years on planet earth because you feel stable, happy, and able.

Listen to how you speak to yourself. Do you talk negatively, calling yourself the names you heard when you were a kid? Or do you tell yourself that you are good and worthwhile?

At first, it may seem awkward self-parenting, but with practice, you can not only contact your wounded inner child but heal the scars that exist deep down in your psyche.

Here are a few tips to Re-parenting yourself:

- Use positive affirmations such as "I am a good person.
- Talk to your adult self to ask for aid in grown-up decisions
- Give rewards to yourself every day
- Get plenty of sleep

- Write in a Re-parenting notebook a daily to-do list and celebrate when you have completed the tasks
- Practice mindfulness to remain present
- Tell yourself that you love you even if it feels awkward
- Think about the wonderful memories you had in childhood
- Make new "good" memories and traditions

By Re-parenting yourself, you will find a powerful ally who will ever stick with you through thick and thin yourself.

Learning to Love Child Alters

Collectively, child alters also go by the term 'littles.' Littles are alters who are under the age of eight, while middles are ages nine to thirteen, teens ages 13 and 18, and bigs who are adults and older than teens.

Not all alters can fit neatly into one age group or the other as they are sliders, capable of sliding in and out of different age ranges.

Littles, like other alters often have symbolic names that are directly related to their function, such as Thor the protector. Other littles may have names that are related to an event or someone they love or know.

Unfortunately, some littles are given a name related to the perpetrator.

Beginning an Inner Dialogue with Alters

It is critical to remember that the alters, even the child ones, are all you.

I am bound to get some push back from some multiples on this next statement, but it needs to be said. The child alters in your system (or whatever term you have given them) are all parts of the whole you. They are not separate people, nor are they invaders. They are all you.

I say that to begin this article because remembering the previous statement is true is key to overcoming the chaos of DID. You are not magical. They are you, and you are them.

When you speak of a child alter as being fearful, what you are honestly saying is that you are feeling afraid.

Understanding that the parts inside your psyche are not strangers who have invaded you makes it a little easier to open a dialogue with them. These parts of your psyche are children, teens, young adults who need and deserve respect, dignity, and love.

The kicker is, only you can give that to them.

To get to know the child parts of yourself who are all stuck in trauma-time better, it may be necessary to form a safe place in your mind. It can be a warm, sandy beach, a sunny flower-strewn meadow, or the top of a mountain. Whatever works for you and your system is what you need to choose.

There are several reasons for forming this safe place:

- It helps all your parts feel safe
- It allows a place to go when you feel overwhelmed
- It allows a place where you can hold conversations with each other

It is vital to understand that words are mighty things. Words can build up and tear down. Words can affirm or destroy. Words are a potent force for good or for evil.

Understanding these facts will help you know what you should and should not say to your alters, who are all you.

To begin a discussion with inner child parts, first, make sure you are safe. This type of dialogue may require you to be in the presence of a mental health professional, at least at first, until you feel more connected and grounded.

Remember this too. Since an alter is a child, they should be treated as children. Do not talk about huge grown-up topics; instead, meet them where they are and allow yourself to feel their emotions. Always keep in mind that alters may refuse to meet you in your safe place. But, even if they refuse, eventually they will come if you give them a reason to want to.

Once grounded, opening your talk with
some simple questions asked inside your
safe place of your alters. Questions can be as
simple as "What's your name?" or "How old
are you?" Do not expect an answer right at
first because you have most likely been
afraid of your child alters before this day;
they may also be fearful of you.

Some other useful hints for starting an inner
dialogue with alters are:

Welcome Them. Make the first move and
take an interest in the child alter you are
speaking with. Allow them to acclimate to
being with you and set them at ease as much
as you can. You can also tell them how
excited you are to be meeting your alters and
show our enthusiasm and excitement.

Set Boundaries and Rules. One of the best
things about starting an inner dialogue is
that rules and boundaries can be set to assure
that your life becomes more manageable.
Rules such as child alters in your system
may not overwhelm you with flashbacks,
and boundaries such as no cussing (or

whatever you wish) are essential. Children need and love rules, and so do many adults, thus making some for your safe place makes perfect sense.

Use Their Name. Say their name often to establish that you are listening and validating what they are saying. Obviously, this hint only works if you know the alters name.

Offer to Help. Your inner child parts are there because something horrid happened to you in childhood. They hold all the memories and secrets of what occurred and are in pain. If you offer your inner child parts help, such as telling them you are going to protect them now, they will grow in trust as time goes by.

Listen. By listening more than you speak, you will learn much from your alters. They will let you in on their hopes and dreams, which, of course, are what you wanted when you were their age.

Feel. Feel the emotions from needs that were not met in your childhood. It is okay to weep over what was torn from you in the past.

Enjoy Your Inner Children

The child parts of you that live in your mind are loveable and enjoyable if you give them half a chance. They are all delightful parts of you stuck in trauma-time that need to be loved and cared for so you can heal.

Even the members of your system who have caused you problems in the past or who act hostile are only acting out because they have unmet needs.

Self-parenting means giving to your inner child selves the dignity, respect, and love that they deserve, and you will provide these vital human needs to yourself. It may frighten at first, but with practice, you find you look forward to going to your safe place to meet the beautiful pieces that make up you.

References

Alters in Dissociative Identity Disorder. (Aug 30, 2021). Traumadissociation.com. Retrieved Aug 30, 2021. from http://traumadissociation.com/alters.

American Psychiatric Association. (2013). Diagnostic and statistical manual of mental disorders: DSM-5. (5th ed.). Washington, D.C.: American Psychiatric Association. ISBN 0890425558.

Braun, Bennett G. (1986). Treatment of Multiple Personality Disorder. American Psychiatric Pub, ISBN 0880480963.

Dean, M. (2020). Inner Child: What Is It, What Happened to It, And How Can I Fix It?. *Betterhelp.com.* Retrieved from: https://www.betterhelp.com/advice/therapy/inner-child-what-is-it-what-happened-to-it-and-how-can-i-fix-it/

Del Casale, F., Munilla, H. L., de Del Casale, L. R., & Fullone, E. (1982). Defective parenting and reparenting. *Transactional Analysis Journal,* 12(3), 181–184.

Diagnostic and Statistical Manual of Mental Disorders edition 5. American Psychiatric Association, (2013).

Haddock D, (2001). The Dissociative Identity Disorder Sourcebook. McGraw-Hill, ISBN 0737303948.

International Society for the Study of Trauma and Dissociation. (2011). [Chu, J. A., Dell, P. F., Van der Hart, O., Cardeña, E., Barach, P. M., Somer, E., Loewenstein, R. J., Brand, B., Golston, J. C., Courtois, C. A., Bowman, E. S., Classen, C., Dorahy, M., Sar,V., Gelinas,D.J., Fine,C.G., Paulsen, S., Kluft, R. P., Dalenberg, C. J., Jacobson-Levy, M., Nijenhuis, E. R. S., Boon, S., Chefetz, R.A., Middleton, W., Ross, C. A., Howell, E., Goodwin, G., Coons, P. M., Frankel, A. S., Steele, K., Gold, S. N., Gast, U., Young, L. M., & Twombly, J.]. Guidelines for treating dissociative identity disorder in adults, third revision.Journal of Trauma & Dissociation, 12, 115–187. Doi: 10.1080/15299732.2011.537247.

James, Muriel (1998). "Self-reparenting and redecision." *Transactional Analysis Journal*. **28**: 16–19

Kneisl, C. R. (1991). Healing the wounded, neglected inner child of the past. The Nursing Clinics of North America, 26(3), 745-755.

Luna, A. 25 Signs you have a wounded inner child (and how to heal). Retrieved from: https://lonerwolf.com/feeling-safe-inner-child/

Moroney, Margaret (1989). "Comparison of 5 methods". Transactional Analysis Journal. 19: 35–41.

Osnes, Russell (1974). "Spot reparenting." *Transactional Analysis Journal*. **4** (3): 40–46.

Öztürk, E., & Sar, V. (2016). Formation and functions of alter personalities in dissociative identity disorder: A theoretical and clinical elaboration. *J Psychol Clin Psychiatry*, 6(6), 00385.

Teicher, M. H., & Samson, J. A. (2016). Annual research review: enduring neurobiological effects of childhood abuse and neglect. Journal of child psychology and psychiatry, 57(3), 241-266.

Wikipedia. Reparenting. Retrieved from: https://en.wikipedia.org/wiki/Reparenting#Total_Regression

Lists of Links to Helpful Websites

https://www.nurseslearning.com/courses/nrp/NRP-1618/Section%205/index.htm

http://traumadissociation.com/alters

https://did-research.org/did/alters/ages

https://www.havoca.org/survivors/dissociative-identity-disorder/alters/